Revealing the Golden Rules of Social Media Advertising

Table of Contents

Your culture is your brand.

— Tony Hsieh

Chapter 1. Introduction

Get ready to dive into the thrilling world of online marketing with our Special Report: "Revealing the Golden Rules of Social Media Advertising"! This illuminating guide will unleash the secrets to truly effective social media advertising, regardless of your business size or the platforms you're using. Equip yourself with the enticing strategies, attention-grabbing techniques, and effective campaign management tips that leading marketers swear by. Each page you turn will beam with innovative and handy guidelines, turning all your posts into impressions gold. So why wait? Begin your joyous journey towards social media advertising mastery and watch your business fly to newer heights. Embark, explore, and enjoy!

Chapter 2. The Dawn of Social Media Advertising

As we take a strategic dive into the vast ocean of social media advertising, our first perturbation takes us to its beginning. A pristine era where exchanges evolved from physical meet and greets to digital interactions, redefining businesses and personal relationships, paving the way to the powerful medium we have come to know today.

2.1. Emergence of Social Media

The inception of social media can be tracked back to the late 1990s', with small but vital platforms such as Six Degrees and Blogger. Additions to the domain like Friendster and Myspace in the early 2000s, although popular, fell short of exploiting the advertising potential that social media possessed. This demarcates the transition phase from physical to digital platforms. The real game-changer was Facebook, in the year 2004. Their omnipresence made them a frontrunner in data gathering, leading to unbelievably precise targeted advertising. Other platforms such as Twitter, Instagram, YouTube followed suit, further expanding the digital horizon.

2.2. The Rise of Ads on Social Media

In the beginning, ads were displayed on social networks as humble banner ads, primarily on Myspace. However, observing the growing popularity, businesses saw the potential for advertising on these platforms. In 2007, Facebook launched 'Social Ads', marking the birth of truly social media advertising. With time, other platforms such as Twitter and LinkedIn also introduced their own advertising facets. As social media cultivated data-rich environments, the spectrum for personalized advertising amplified. The ability to target audiences based on demographics, geography, interests, and behavior became a reality.

2.3. Evolution of Social Media Advertising

Since its inception, social media advertising has seen more than a fair share of evolution. From plain text ads to rich media, the transformation has been outstanding. The integration of analytics, ad-tech, and programmatic buying refined the process further. Moreover, platforms introduced new features like auto-play videos, carousel ads, dynamic product ads, etc., to enhance the ad experience.

2.4. Social Media Advertising and the Mobile Revolution

By 2014, the switch to mobile was inescapable. The increasing usage of smartphones catalyzed this shift. Social networks adapted their advertising mechanisms to fit the mobile platform, adding features like location-based advertising. Mobile advertising on social media became so crucial that platforms redesigned their products from a "mobile-first" perspective.

2.5. Data Mining and Its Impact

Data has been at the heart of social media advertising. It helped personalize the ad experience, making it more effective. Machine learning algorithms learned from past data to predict user preferences and streamline ad delivery. Even the rise of privacy and data breaches couldn't deter the spirit of online marketing as algorithms became adept at personalization, without violating user privacy.

2.6. Social Media Advertising Today

Currently, social media advertising stands tall as an indispensable ingredient of any online marketing strategy. The integration of AI and AR/VR technologies is transforming the domain, taking personalization to a wholly new level. Real-time interaction, predictive analysis, influencers, and ephemeral content form the crux of modern-day social media advertising.

Indeed, the dawn of social media advertising was a revelation, an era bestowed with possibilities. The subsequent chapters of this guide delve into the in-depth exploration of these possibilities; educating you on the techniques and strategies to harness the full potential of social media advertising, leading your business to newer heights of success. Thus, as we leave the break of dawn behind, we tread into the beautiful day that awaits us, ready to unravel layer after layer of the multi-faceted world of social media advertising.

Chapter 3. Understanding Your Target Audience

Our exploration of the world of social media advertising commences with one crucial precept: understanding your target audience. No successful marketing or advertising strategy can ever truly take off without a clear, comprehensive understanding of who you are marketing to. This step functions as the bedrock foundation upon which you build your advertising initiatives, shaping the content, timing, frequency, and choice of social media platform.

3.1. The Importance of Demographics

Demographics entail the statistical data concerning the characteristics of population groups. They are fundamental to any marketing strategy, particularly in the realm of social media advertising, where the sheer volume and diversity of users necessitates a tapered focus to ensure your advertising efforts produce the desired outcomes. Demographics can include, but are not limited to, factors such as age, gender, economic status, educational level, and geographical location.

Understand that different demographics have preferences for different social media platforms. For instance, younger audiences (aged 18-24) gravitate towards platforms like Instagram and TikTok, while Facebook and LinkedIn are more popular among older users. The timing and content of your advertisements must be curated with these demographic realities in mind.

3.2. The Significance of Psychographics

While demographics lay down a solid groundwork, they only provide a partial view of the landscape. That's where psychographics come in. Psychographics pry open the door into your target audience's minds, giving you insight into their attitudes, personal interests, values, hobbies, lifestyles, and behavioral patterns. The crux of psychographics is: it tells you why your audience behaves the way they do.

Knowing your audience's motivations can empower you to create content that resonates with them on a deeper level. Harnessing this information will enable you to craft ad content that can strike an emotional chord or speak to their specific needs and pain points, increasing the likelihood they will engage with your ad and, in turn, your goods or services.

3.3. Sociographics Matter too

Sociographics seamlessly marry demographics and psychographics. Sociographics track how individuals interact within a community, their roles within groups - both social and professional, and how these interactions influence their behavior. This snapshot of the social climate is pivotal when trying to translate blanket audience understanding into a focused social media strategy.

Using sociographics, you can tweak your ad strategies to appeal to group dynamics and community interests. For instance, if you find out through research that your target audience is concerned with environmental sustainability, you could create a campaign that showcases your company's dedication to green initiatives.

3.4. Leveraging Social Media Data

Social media platforms are a treasure trove of data, with each interaction serving as a window into your audience's habits, preferences, and online behaviors.

Rely on these platforms' native analytics tools. Instagram insights, Facebook analytics, and Twitter Analytics provide much-needed information on who your audience is, the kind of content they like, what times they are most active, and how they interact with different kinds of content. By harnessing such data, you can tailor your advertising strategy to meet your audience's needs and preferences effectively.

3.5. Conducting Market Research

Successful advertisers can't afford to ride solely on the coattails of hunches or suppositions. They must back up their strategies with robust, data-driven market research. Primary market research methods like surveys, interviews, focus groups, and observations can glean first-hand information about your target audience and its needs, wants, and purchasing behaviors. Secondary market research includes reviewing existing research and data, gaining a broader understanding of market conditions and potential opportunities.

3.6. Constructing Buyer Personas

To actualize the data gathered through demographics, psychographics, sociographics, social media data, and market research, it's necessary to create detailed buyer personas. A buyer persona is a fictional, yet concrete and fact-backed representation of your ideal customer. This persona should be reflective of the data on hand, and may also include additional details such as job status, digital habits, and purchasing behavior.

Creating buyer personas makes your data more palatable, allowing you to keep these personas in mind when crafting your advertising strategy. Advertising with a specific persona in mind ensures your content is not generic and can connect with its intended audience.

Undeniably, understanding your target audience is an exercise of equal parts science and intuition. As you delve deeper into their personalities, habits, and lifestyle choices, you'll be better positioned to foster an engaging, effective, and ultimately successful social media advertising strategy. While this process is daunting and time-consuming, the rewards of a deeply researched and intricately crafted strategy are immeasurable and invaluable.

Chapter 4. Choosing the Right Social Media Platform for Advertising

Just as every business is unique, so too are the social media platforms at their disposal. Choosing the right platform for social media marketing lays the groundwork for future success, and understanding the function, strengths, and user base of each platform is the first step on this momentous journey. The correct platform can serve as a magnet, drawing customer attention and facilitating engagement. Neglecting or misinterpreting these nuances may result in undermining the very goal of your marketing efforts.

4.1. Analyzing Different Social Media Platforms

Before arriving at a decision, explore and comprehend the nuances of various social media platforms in terms of their demographics, preferences, and most importantly - their engagement patterns.

Let's examine some of the most popular platforms:

- *Facebook*: With over 2 billion active users monthly, Facebook constitutes the biggest social media platform. Its user base spans all age groups, creating a variety of opportunities for businesses of all sizes. Equipped with extensive targeting features including location, age, language, and interests, Facebook ads allow businesses to reach their exact target audience, making this platform suitable for B2C businesses.

- *Instagram*: Instagram, owned by Facebook, targets younger audiences, with 67% of its users being under the age of 35. Instagram's visual focus makes it a perfect platform for brands that rely heavily on images such as retail and luxury goods. It offers photo and video advertisements, shopping features, and IGTV for longer video content.

- *Twitter*: This fast-paced platform has a user base of 330 million, popular among university graduates and people earning high incomes. Businesses can share short messages (known as tweets) and include relevant hashtags in their posts to boost visibility. Twitter is especially suited for influencer marketing efforts.

- *LinkedIn*: LinkedIn is the leading B2B social media platform. It's a powerful tool for businesses to reach professionals and job seekers. It allows precise targeting by position, job title, company, and even skills.

4.2. Aligning Your Business Goals and Audience Needs

Recognizing the unique characteristics of each platform ensures alignment with your business goals and audience needs. Therefore, determining the ideal platform requires an understanding of the objectives and target audience of your campaign. We illustrate this process through an example:

Imagine you have a high-end jewelry company. Your target audience is likely to be older, wealthy women interested in fashion and luxury goods. After careful evaluation, you might conclude that the majority of your target audience uses Facebook and Instagram, so these platforms could be beneficial for your ad campaign.

Likewise, if you're in B2B marketing looking to reach senior-level executives, LinkedIn might be your platform of choice due to its professional user base.

4.3. Evaluating Platform Capabilities

Various platforms offer different advertisement capabilities. Some channels provide detailed targeting options, robust analytics, and a variety of ad formats. Evaluating these capabilities can significantly influence your platform decision. For instance, if your ad campaign heavily relies on video content, you might opt for Facebook or YouTube as both provide sophisticated video ad support. Alternatively, if your strategy involves keyword targeting, a platform like Twitter could be beneficial due to its emphasis on real-time discussion and trending hashtags.

In addition, consider the cost of advertising on each platform. Some platforms may require higher bids or offer lower ad impressions at the same cost as another platform. Evaluating your budget alongside these variables can aid in making a strategic decision.

4.4. Leveraging the Power of Multi-Platform Advertising

The strategies mentioned earlier do not advocate for a mono-platform approach. Each platform offers unique benefits and using more than one can help in balancing your advertising strategy. Utilizing a multi-platform approach can diversify your reach, preventing overdependence on a single platform.

Understanding which platforms your target audience spends the most time on, coupled with the ability to tailor your ads to those platforms, will significantly improve the ability of your advertisements to engage, attract, and convert potential consumers. Leveraging multiple platforms can maximize your reach and ad spend, driving better ROI and enabling a holistic social media advertising strategy.

In conclusion, choosing the right social media platform for your advertising needs is a multifaceted process, and doing so effectively requires a deep understanding of various platform attributes, your business goals, and the characteristics of your target audience. By dissecting and analyzing these fundamental components of social media advertising, you can make informed decisions that will ultimately drive your marketing success.

Chapter 5. Crafting Captivating Ad Content

Crafting captivating ad content is arguably one of the kindred spirit tasks of any successful social media advertising campaign. Excellent ad content engages, informs, intrigues, and motivates users towards your intended action. It's not only about the phenomenal ideas, but also the compelling ways they are conveyed. Remember, with a myriad of brand messages competing for your target audience's attention span, your ad content must shine like a beacon in a sea of sameness.

5.1. The Art of Storytelling

On social media platforms, storytelling is the key to winning hearts. Stories can be personal, emotional, funny, or surprising. They stimulate empathy and engagement and connect your brand to potential customers on a deeper level. To weave the perfect story around your ad content:

- Ensure it aligns with the desires or pain points of your audience.
- Project your main message or product feature in the narrative.
- Make the story powerful yet relatable.
- Don't forget to incorporate the proper call-to-action (CTA).

5.2. Visual Allure: Graphics, Photos, and Videos

The second facet of crafting alluring ad content lies within its visual presentation. It's completely substantiated that the human brain processes visual information much faster than textual information.

That's where graphics, images, and videos come into play. A captivating illustration or an attention-grabbing video can contribute to half the success of your ad campaign.

- Use high-quality images or animated graphics for your ads.
- Match imagery or footage with the story or concept of the ad.
- Ensure your visuals convey the same message as your text for coherence.
- Making use of colours that align with your brand identity ensures consistency.

5.3. Appealing Ad Copies

An effective ad copy is equally as important as a captivating story or an appealing visual element. Your ad copy should be engaging and interest-provoking, easily understandable, succinct, and on-point.

- Craft clear and concise copies. Shorter sentences are easier to comprehend.
- Use action-oriented words to guide users through what you want them to do.
- Inject words that trigger emotions. Emotional appeals often result in action.
- Implement persuasive writing techniques to convince and convert.

5.4. Call-to-Actions (CTAs) that Work

A powerful CTA propels action – it is the button that audience members click to take advantage of an offer, learn something new, discover something they're interested in, or make a purchase. Your CTAs must be clear, compelling and evoke the urgency or scarcity concept well.

- Ensure your CTA is simple yet enticing.

- Use strong action verbs - 'Download', 'Sign-up', 'Visit', etc.

- Convey urgency or scarcity - 'Limited offer', 'Only a few left', etc.

- Locate your CTAs prominently and make them visually appealing.

5.5. Written Content: Blogs, Whitepapers, eBooks

Long-form content, like blogs, whitepapers, and eBooks, brings substantial value when your objective goes beyond immediate conversion. Such content is designed to aid in educating your customers, guiding them through a problem, or facilitating better understanding of a topic that is tightly bound to your product or service.

- Position your brand as an industry expert by generating insightful, instructional content.

- Encourage audience participation through questions and surveys.

- Utilize keywords and SEO techniques to ensure better visibility on search engines.

- Promote your content widely through your social media platforms and encourage shares.

In conclusion, crafting captivating ad content for social media advertising is about understanding your audience, telling a story that resonates, using compelling visuals, creating engaging ad copies and CTAs, and intelligently incorporating long-form written content. It's about the harmonious blend of all these elements that results in ad content that compels, converts, and creates lasting brand impressions.

Chapter 6. Mastering Ad Timing and Frequency

Comprehending the principles of timing and frequency in advertising campaigns, particularly those disseminated through social media platforms, is tantamount to unlocking the door to optimally engaging with your target audience. These components grant you the power to strategically position your content exactly when your audience is most active and receptive. In this chapter, we'll unravel the plush intricacies of ad scheduling, delving into the most auspicious times to post, how often you should do it, and ways to curate a posting schedule that complements your unique business needs and customer behavior patterns.

6.1. The Relevance of Timing in Ad Deployment

Let's first embark on discussing the importance of timing in advertisement broadcasting. A well-timed social media advertisement is akin to an expertly honed arrow, striking the bulls-eye at exactly the right moment. Comprehending when your audience is most likely to be active and engaging with content will amplify the ad's reach, visibility, and potential for user engagement. Without cognizant application of time-specific strategies, your adverts might disappear in the ceaseless tide of posts churned out by other businesses on social media platforms. As such, it becomes imperative to discern the ideal hour to broadcast your ad for maximized visibility and engagement.

6.2. Frequency: Striking a Harmonious Balance

Equally significant as timing is the frequency of your ad posts—the quantity of times your advertisement is shown to the same user over a specified period. Here lies the delicate dance of balance; too frequent, and you risk annoying or desensitizing your audience to your content, causing ad fatigue. Too infrequent, and they may not have ample opportunity to register and respond to your message. There's a fine line between saturation and scarcity, so modulating the frequency based on your ad's specificity, audience characteristics, and platform guidelines can guide your raft along this tricky ripple of digital advertisement.

6.3. In Pursuit of the Perfect Timing

Ascertaining the perfect time to post on social media platforms necessitates rigorous comprehension of your audience's online behavior. Different platforms cater to diverse user demographics, equating to variations in peak activity times. For instance, business professionals may be more active on LinkedIn during the start and end of the workday, while Instagram's younger demographic may grant higher engagement rates post-school hours or late evenings. Using insights tools offered by these platforms, you can access invaluable data regarding your audience's most active hours, thereby optimizing your ad timing.

6.4. Frequency and Audience Fatigue

Ad frequency should be adjusted with caution, bearing in mind the potential onset of audience fatigue. This is a phenomenon where individuals, after seeing the same ad repetitively in a short duration, grow unresponsive or develop negative perceptions towards the advertiser. To combat this, implement ad rotation strategies, diversifying the content while maintaining the core message and branding. This way, your audience stays engaged, and fatigue is kept at bay.

6.5. Scheduling Advertisements: The Pathway to Precision

Creating and sticking to an ad schedule is your key to the kingdom of precise timing and frequency. Evaluate your objectives, audience's active hours, resources at disposal, and ad content diversity to devise a schedule that reflects a harmonious blend of these factors. Remember, consistency is key. Maintaining a regular schedule reassures the audience of your brand's reliability, and also paves the way towards improved organic reach and potential virality.

6.6. Decoding Metrics: The Gauge for Success

Lastly, the measures of success aren't merely intuitive or observational. They are data-driven and quantifiable. Monitor metrics reflecting ad performance such as reach, impressions, engagement rate, and frequency to continually fine-tune your approach. Keeping a keen eye on these figures helps you identify trends, peak periods, anomalies or potential adjacency, translating into informed decisions concerning future ad timing and frequency adjustments.

Social media advertising is a dynamic, fluid domain. To remain effective and competitive, the careful orchestration of ad timing and frequency is indispensable, requiring continuous adjustment and refinement. Armed with the guidelines and strategies discussed, you can now proceed to master this aspect of social media advertising and craft an impactful, effective, and engaging presence for your brand online.

Chapter 7. Utilizing SEO in Social Media Advertising

As much as social media advertising is crucial in building your digital presence, combining it with the power of Search Engine Optimization (SEO) can yield results beyond your wildest imagination in driving organic traffic, boosting engagement, and multiplying conversions. This chapter of our treasured guide will delve into this compelling alliance, where social media advertising kisses the charisma of SEO, and how it can add invaluable worth to your campaigns.

7.1. The Confluence of Social Media Advertising and SEO

Understanding how social media advertising interacts with SEO is essential to leverage their combined potential fully. It was a prevalent myth in the realm of digital marketing that social media signals, such as likes, shares, and followers, directly impact search engine rankings. As per Google's formal statements, these factors are not direct ranking signals in their algorithm. Nevertheless, that doesn't make the intersection of SEO and social media advertising insignificant; on the contrary, their indirect influence is far-reaching and powerful.

When you create shareable content on your social media, it enhances its visibility, resulting in increased linking possibilities. More websites may link to your content, which is a significant factor in how Google ranks pages. Moreover, a robust social media presence can help your content get indexed faster. Google also recognizes credible social media profiles, which you can use to your advantage to appear in relevant search results.

7.2. Building an Integrated Strategy

For a harmonious relationship between social media advertising and SEO, you need an integrated strategy that works ceaselessly towards your marketing goals. This strategy should marry your social media advertising objectives such as brand awareness, customer engagement, and conversions, with your SEO goals like improving organic rankings and driving sustainable, long-term traffic.

Key to an integrated strategy is consistency. Consistency in your messaging, voice, branding, and value proposition across your social media networks and SEO efforts helps in improving brand recall and organic visibility. You should strive to use the same keywords and phrases that you aim to rank for in search engine results, in your social media ads as well. Your social media content, advertisements, and engagement efforts should be in tune with your on-site content, blog posts, and other SEO efforts.

7.3. Harnessing the Power of Keywords in Social Media Advertising

Just like SEO relies on strategic keyword usage, infusing your social media advertising with relevant keywords can amplify your visibility. You need to understand what terms your potential customers are using when they search for products or services. Use keyword research tools, audience insights, and analytics to identify these keywords and incorporate them into your social media posts, image alt descriptions, ad copies, hashtags, and even profile bios.

Remember, social media channels also function as search engines where users can 'search' for content. By optimizing your posts and ads with relevant keywords, you can ensure that your offerings appear prominently in these internal search results, leading to enhanced visibility and engagement.

7.4. Capitalizing on the Power of Social Media Profiles

If you have ever performed a Google search of a business, you would have likely noticed that social media profiles are usually among the top results. This visibility is a testament to how search engines value social media profiles. Therefore, it is essential to ensure that your social media profiles are not only active but also optimized for visibility.

Use relevant keywords and hashtags in your profile descriptions and bios. Furnish comprehensive business details including address, hours of operation, contact information, and a link to your website. Regularly post valuable content and engage with your audience. Having well-maintained social media profiles can help you appear more often in relevant search results, and direct more organic traffic to your pages.

7.5. Encouraging Social Sharing for Link-building

Social sharing can be a potent tool for building backlinks, which hold immense SEO value. The more your content gets shared across social networks, the more visibility it gains, and the chances for other websites to link to your content increase.

Encouraging this social sharing can take several forms. You can create valuable, informative and entertaining content that resonates with your audience and urges them to share. You can also sprinkle shareable quotes, infographics, statistics, and images across your content. And let's not forget the power of social share buttons — by strategically placing them around your content, you make it convenient for users to share your content, thus maximizing its spreading potential.

This synergy between social media advertising and SEO is a testament to how various digital marketing disciplines can work in harmony to create amplified results. A strategic fusion of these can lead to an incredibly efficient flywheel, churning out improved visibility, increased organic traffic, and heightened user engagement. In your illustrious journey of social media advertising, this unique intersection will play a crucial role in enabling your campaigns to attain the pinnacle of success. Let SEO boost your social media advertising to soaring heights, uncage new growth leaps and paint a prosperous digital future of your brand.

Chapter 8. Analysis and Interpretation of Ad Performance Data

The journey through social media advertising is as intriguing as it is rewarding. An integral pit stop on this journey involves deciphering the cryptic realm of ad performance data. This chapter aims to demystify the potent world of analytics, guiding you through the process of analyzing and interpreting data obtained from various social media ads.

8.1. The Importance of Data Analysis in Social Media Advertising

In the grand scheme of online advertising, data analytics plays a pivotal role. Developing a successful ad strategy requires understanding ad performance data not just in the context of numbers or statistics, but in the holistic sense of how it practically impacts your advertising outcomes, including viewer engagement, conversions, and ultimately your Return on Investment (ROI). This approach allows you to derive insights about customer behavior and preferences, empowering you to fine-tune your advertising strategy and optimize ad performance.

8.2. Understanding Key Performance Indicators (KPIs)

Your advertising strategy's success banks heavily on identifying the right Key Performance Indicators (KPIs). KPIs, essentially, are measurable values that demonstrate how effectively you are achieving your business objectives. In the realm of social media advertising, these can range from indicators like Click-Through Rates (CTR), Conversion Rate, Cost per Click (CPC), Impressions, or even Page Engagement.

Social media platforms typically offer tools to track these KPIs. Facebook, for instance, offers Facebook Insights, which provides comprehensive data about your page's activities and audience interaction.

8.3. The Art of Data Interpretation

Data interpretation is not merely about analyzing numbers, but also about understanding the story these numbers are trying to tell. Effective data interpretation can led to an enriched marketing strategy, making it potentially more impactful and high-yielding.

For instance, a sudden decrease in your ad's impressions could mean its content is not as compelling anymore. A drop in the click-through rate might indicate a disconnection between your ad's targeting and its message. Conversely, an increase in engagement and conversion rates after a content modification could mean your revamped message resonates better with your audience.

8.4. Tools for Ad Performance Data Analysis

To streamline the process of analysis and interpretation, several analytical tools such as Google Analytics, Hootsuite, SEMrush, and Sprout Social, amongst others, are available at your disposal. Each of these tools caters to different facets of data analysis and interpretation, and their usage is dependent on your specific requirements.

8.5. Effectively Using Analytical Insights

After successful interpretation of the collected data, it's essential to leverage these insights to enhance your advertising strategy. This could manifest as tweaks to the content, alteration in ad frequency timing, upscaling the ad spend based on ROI, or even overhauling your entire social media advertising plan.

The issue often faced in this task is not the lack of data, rather an overflow. How to effectively navigate this ocean and fish out the most relevant data chunks forms the crux of a successful social media ad campaign.

8.6. Learning from Mistakes

Ad campaigns will not always yield the desired results, despite the best laid plans. What's pivotal is interpreting these failures as learning opportunities rather than setbacks. A data-driven approach can reveal where the strategy missed the mark, whether in terms of content, placement, timing, or targeting.

Social media advertising is a riveting journey of trial and error, punctuated by analytical insights. Collaborating cogent analysis with the interpretation of ad performance data is like assembling a massive jigsaw puzzle, with each piece playing a crucial role in creating the complete, successful ad campaign picture. And when all these pieces fall into place, the fruition is indeed a sight to behold for any visionary, data-driven marketer.

Chapter 9. Budget Allocation: Maximizing Ad Spend and ROI

In this era of technological advancement, where online platforms are quickly transforming the face of marketing, it's important to strategically allocate resources to maximize the effectiveness of your social media advertisements. This core chapter delves into the wisdom behind superior budget allocation, making the most out of your ad spend, and achieving optimal Return On Investment (ROI).

9.1. Understanding the Importance of Budget Allocation

Budget allocation is the process of assigning a specific amount of resources to different components of your marketing plan, including social media advertising. It's imperative to give serious thought to this stage in your strategic planning, ensuring that your financial resources are invested wisely.

Each social media platform has a unique pay structure, and you must account for these differing costs when allocating your budget. Not only that, but each platform offers distinct features and caters to diverse demographics, all of which calls for careful consideration whilst distributing your budget.

However, proper budget allocation extends beyond spreading your resources across different platforms; it's about strategically investing your funds in a way that approimately pursues the business's vision and mission. Through meticulously calculated budget allocation, you could see your ad spend convert into a goldmine of profitability and growth, yielding an impressive ROI.

9.2. Keys to Effective Budget Allocation

When allocating your budget, consider these four key aspects:

Understanding Your Business Goals: Define what you hope to achieve through your social media advertising campaigns. Are you aiming for increased brand awareness or are you driving sales? The answer will guide your financial allocation decisions.

The Performance of Your Previous Ad Campaigns: Evaluate the success of your past advertising campaigns on different social media platforms. Take into account metrics like engagement rate, cost per click (CPC), and conversion rates.

Target Audience: The platform choice should be predominantly driven by where your customers spend the majority of their online time. Tailor your budget allocation to reach the largest fraction of your target audience possible.

Ad Content and Formats: Certain content types or ad formats may perform better in terms of cost-effectiveness than others. Consider these factors whilst allocating your funds.

9.3. Methods to Maximize Ad Spend

Once you've laid down a robust framework for your budget allocation, it's time to explore methods to make the most out of your ad spend. Consider:

Using Custom and Lookalike Audiences: Platforms like Facebook and Instagram allow you to target custom audiences (users who have already interacted with your brand) and lookalike audiences (users similar to your existing customers). This can significantly improve the effectiveness of your ads.

Investing in High-Performing Posts: Monitor your organic content and identify posts with high engagement. Allocate additional ad spend to promote these messages to a wider audience.

Optimizing Ad Schedules: Study your audience's online behavior. Schedule your ads for when your target audience is likely to be online to gain maximum visibility.

9.4. Determining Return On Investment (ROI)

Monitoring the ROI on your ad spend is essential as it offers insights into your campaign's financial performance. The most common way to calculate ROI is by using the formula: ROI = (Net Profit / Cost of Investment) x 100

Measuring ROI can help identify which campaigns are bringing the most returns and which ones may need readjusting. It also helps in future budget allocation and ad campaign planning.

9.5. Case Study: Effective Budget Allocation

Let's unriddle the power of strategic budget allocation with an example. An online retail store spent $1,000 on social media advertising. Through meticulous demographic analysis, they allocated $600 to Facebook, $200 to Instagram, and $200 to LinkedIn. Their efforts resulted in $3500 worth of sales. The ROI would be: ((3500 - 1000) / 1000) x 100 = 250%, meaning for every $1 invested, they made $2.50 back.

This chapter brought to light the essentials of smart budget allocation, maximizing ad spend, and gauging ROI in social media advertising. As you continue your journey through this guide, remember that the key to uncovering the treasure-trove of successful online advertising lies in understanding, planning, analyzing, and adjusting your strategies to conquer the multifaceted world of social media advertising.

Chapter 10. A/B Testing: The Process of Refinement

A/B testing, also known as split testing, is a methodological approach in marketing that can significantly enhance the efficiency of your social media advertising efforts. This chapter will provide a meticulous explanation of A/B testing, outlining its importance, methods, benefits, and real-life application cases.

10.1. Understanding A/B Testing

A/B testing is a technique where two variants of a webpage, ad, or another marketing asset are pitted against each other to determine which performs better. Variant A acts as the control, the original version, while Variant B features certain changes aimed at improving results. Your audience is separated into two groups for the test, with one seeing Variant A and the other seeing Variant B. The key metrics of both are then measured and compared.

10.2. The Importance of A/B Testing

Without testing, it's impossible to know what works best for your specific audience. Assumptions can sometimes lead to wasted resources or even detrimental results. A/B testing alleviates these risks by providing data-driven conclusions about what's effective and what's not. It allows marketers to make informed decisions based on empirical evidence rather than guesswork.

10.3. Setting Up A/B Tests in Social Media Advertising

The fundamental steps to setting up an A/B test are: defining the goal, selecting the variable to test, creating the variants, deciding on the sample size, running the test, and analyzing the results. It's essential to only test one variable at a time to clearly understand the influence of that particular change.

Whether you want to increase click-through rates, boost conversions, or improve engagement, setting a definitive goal for the A/B testing is the starting point. This goal becomes your benchmark for measuring the test's success.

The next step involves choosing the to-be-tested variable. It could be the ad's headline, image, call-to-action, or even the timing of the post. You then create two versions of the ad – Variant A and Variant B – with one differing element.

Finally, you decide the audience size for the test and let it run for a suitable period for the results to be statistically valid.

10.4. The Intricacies of Test Analysis

Once your test has run its course, it's time to dive into the results. This part requires a firm understanding of statistical significance and confidence levels. If your test shows that Variant B has a 15% higher conversion rate than Variant A, analyze the result to ensure that this isn't due to chance.

If your results are statistically significant, you should feel confident implementing the changes tested in Variant B more widely. A positive result can result in enhanced ad performance and ultimately a better return on your advertising investment.

10.5. Pitfalls of A/B Testing and How to Avoid Them

While A/B testing is a powerful tool, certain pitfalls can skew your results if not properly understood and avoided. Running multiple tests simultaneously, not considering external factors, or not allowing the test to run for a valid time period are common mistakes.

To avoid these, it's crucial to control the testing environment as much as possible. Limit your tests to one variable at a time, account for external aspects that might impact results, and give your tests enough time to gather a sufficient amount of data.

10.6. A/B Testing in Practice: Real-Life Cases

Several businesses have seen their ad campaigns transform post a successful A/B testing process. A retail chain, for example, saw a 45% increase in their conversion rate just by changing their call to action after conducting an A/B test. Another business drastically cut its CPC (Cost per Click) by optimizing their headline based on insights derived from A/B testing.

A/B testing is not merely an optional practice but a cornerstone in successful social media advertising. It represents an ongoing process of refinement, always searching for the optimal ad versions to meet your defined marketing objectives.

While robust and exhaustive, this chapter merely scratches the surface of A/B testing. We recommend further in-depth study and practice to fully utilize this powerful optimization method in your social media advertising strategy. The secret to a truly effective ad lies not just in creating a good ad, but in continuous refinement through empirical learning, a process where A/B testing plays a linchpin role.

Chapter 11. Case Studies: Success Stories in Social Media Advertising

Much can be learnt from the experiences of those who have walked the path before us, and the realm of social media advertising is no exception. Through this final chapter, we shall embark on a comprehensive and enlightening study of several illustrious instances of successful social media advertising campaigns. These narratives are amplified with methodical analysis and valuable conclusions drawn from each case, to provide an extensive source of learning for your forthcoming social media advertising endeavors.

11.1. Exploring the Success Metrics

Before we delve into these intriguing case studies, it would be prudent to clarify the metrics used to gauge the success of a social media advertising campaign. These key performance indicators (KPIs) include, but are not limited to, reach or impressions, engagement rates, click-through rates (CTR), conversion rates, acquisition costs, return on ad spend (ROAS), and incrementality. By comprehending these metrics, the understanding and interpretation of the case studies presented herein shall become an exponentially more fruitful exercise.

11.2. Airbnb: The Art of Community Building

Airbnb, the global vacation rental marketplace, launched its 'Live There' campaign on Facebook and Instagram. Designed to encourage travelers to "live like a local," the campaign used visually compelling cinemagraphs featuring listings and local experiences. The ad content was personalized based on users' travel preferences, which fostered a strong sense of exclusivity and personal connection. Airbnb reported a 98% increase in bookings, significantly higher click-through rates, and substantial growth in app installations. Through this campaign, Airbnb has shown us the power of personalization in social media advertising and the potential of strategic audience targeting to generate impressive results.

11.3. Spotify: Leveraging User Data for Personalization

Spotify, the popular music streaming platform, unveiled its global 'Wrapped' campaign on multiple social media channels at the end of 2019. The campaign utilized user data to craft a personalized musical summary of the year for each user, which was shareable on social media. The 'Wrapped' campaign drove a high volume of engagement on social media and showcased Spotify's mastering of data analytics. The takeaway here lies in the potential for user data to be leveraged for personalization, driving stronger user engagement and enhancing brand loyalty.

11.4. Old Spice: Turning Viral into a Virtue

Old Spice, a renowned personal care brand, introduced its 'The Man Your Man Could Smell Like' campaign on YouTube. The humorous and witty videos quickly went viral, gaining millions of views, and the company's subscriber count skyrocketed. The simple yet witty content infused with humor was the winning permutation behind the campaign's success. This enlightening case sheds light on the importance of leveraging virality in social media advertising, using captivating and entertaining content to enhance brand recognition and consumer love.

11.5. Nike: Building Social Movement with Powerful Narratives

Nike's inspiring 'Dream Crazy' campaign, featuring Colin Kaepernick, was launched on Twitter. The campaign centered around a powerful narrative, promoting the inspirational message of "Believing in something, even if it means sacrificing everything". Notwithstanding the controversy it generated, the campaign recalibrated Nike's brand image and led to an increase in their sales, exhibiting the strength of a strong narrative even amidst controversies. The primary learning from this case involves harnessing the power of social issues and powerful narratives to create engaging and dynamic social media ads that resonate deeply with audiences.

11.6. LEGO: Merging Offline Activities with Online Engagement

LEGO's #BuildTogether Instagram campaign aimed to encourage families to bond over building LEGO sets during the daunting times of lockdown due to the pandemic. The campaign was fruitful in massively boosting the brand's engagement rates and followers on Instagram. LEGO managed to merge offline activities with online engagement beautifully, demonstrating the possibility of synchronizing offline and online actions to create an innovative and integrated user experience.

Revisiting these success stories, we grasp the inherent truth that, while different strategies worked for different brands, they all had some common elements: meaningful content, creativity, a strong narrative, understanding of their target audiences, and efficient use of data. Therefore, as we conclude this chapter, remember to incorporate the golden insights gleaned from these case studies into your social media advertising strategy, while crafting your unique path to success. Like the brands analyzed above, may your business too build its own compelling success story!